United States General Accounting Office

GAO

Testimony

Before the Subcommittee on Oversight and Investigations, Committee on Veterans' Affairs, House of Representatives

I0411091

For Release on Delivery
Expected at
10 a.m. EDT
Thursday,
September 21, 2000

VA INFORMATION TECHNOLOGY

Progress Continues Although Vulnerabilities Remain

Statement of Joel C. Willemssen
Director, Civil Agencies Information Systems
Accounting and Information Management Division

GAO
Accountability * Integrity * Reliability

GAO/T-AIMD-00-321

Mr. Chairman and Members of the Subcommittee:

Thank you for inviting us to participate in today's hearing on the Department of Veterans Affairs' (VA) information technology (IT) program. As requested, my testimony today will focus on the status of VA's efforts to

- improve its process for selecting, controlling, and evaluating IT investments;

- fill the chief information officer (CIO) position;

- develop an overall strategy for reengineering its business processes;

- complete a departmentwide integrated systems architecture;

- track its IT expenditures;

- implement the Veterans Health Administration's (VHA) Decision Support System and the Veterans Benefits Administration's (VBA) compensation and pension replacement project; and

- improve the department's computer security.

Taken together, these seven areas represent critically important challenges that VA needs to fully address in its information technology journey.

Results in Brief

Overall, VA's IT investment decision-making process has improved, and it has started to implement recommendations we enumerated in May[1] and August[2] of this year. Further, VA is obtaining a full-time CIO now that the Administration has identified a candidate for the position. However, the department no longer plans to develop an overall strategy for reengineering its business processes to effectively function as "One VA," nor, has it defined the integrated IT architecture needed to efficiently acquire and utilize information systems across VA. In addition, VA lacks a

---

[1]*Information Technology: Update on VA Actions to Implement Critical Reforms* (GAO/T-AIMD-00-74, May 11, 2000).

[2]*Information Technology: VA Actions Needed to Implement Critical Reforms* (GAO/AIMD-00-226, August 16, 2000).

uniform mechanism that readily tracks IT expenditures. Instead, VA's different offices use various mechanisms for tracking IT expenditures.

VHA's Decision Support System (DSS) and VBA's compensation and pension replacement project continue to face challenges. As demonstrated in a survey to all Veterans Integrated Service Networks (VISN)[3] and medical centers directors, DSS is not being fully utilized. In addition, while VBA plans to pilot test portions of its compensation and pension replacement system in January 2001, other key issues need to be addressed before the system can be fully implemented. For example, VBA does not have a plan or schedule for converting data from the old system to the new system and exchanging data between the new system and other systems.

Finally, regarding computer security, VA has begun to address weaknesses identified by us and its Office of Inspector General. But until it develops and implements a comprehensive, coordinated security management program, VA will have limited assurance that financial information and sensitive medical records are adequately protected from misuse, unauthorized disclosure, and/or destruction.

Background

The department's vision of "One VA" was articulated to assist it in carrying out its mission of providing benefits and other services to veterans and dependents. It stems from the recognition that veterans think of VA as a single entity, but often encounter a confusing, bureaucratic maze of uncoordinated programs—such as those handling benefits, health care, and burials—that puts them through repetitive and frustrating administrative procedures and delays. According to the department, the "One VA" vision describes how it will use IT in versatile new ways to improve services and enable VA employees to help customers more quickly and effectively—in short, to really become "One VA."

To help carry out its activities, VA plans to spend about $1.4 billion of its total fiscal year 2001 budget of about $48 billion on various IT initiatives. Of this $1.4 billion, about $763 million, $80 million, and $400,000, respectively, are intended for VHA, VBA, and the National Cemetery Administration (NCA). The remaining $589 million is for VA-wide IT initiatives in the financial management, human resources, infrastructure, security, architecture, and planning areas.

---

[3]VHA is comprised of 22 VISNs, which are regional organizations encompassing medical centers, nursing homes, and domiciliaries.

The Clinger-Cohen Act and other related legislative reforms provide guidance on how agencies should plan, manage, and acquire IT as part of their overall information resources management responsibilities. These reforms require agencies to (1) appoint CIOs responsible for providing leadership in acquiring and managing IT resources, (2) perform business process reengineering prior to acquiring new IT, and (3) complete an integrated architecture to guide and constrain future investments.

VA's IT Investment Decision-making Has Improved

The Clinger-Cohen Act requires agency heads to implement an approach for maximizing the value and assessing and managing the risks of IT investments. It stipulates that this approach should be integrated with the agency's budget, financial, and program management processes. As detailed in our investment guide,[4] an IT investment process is an integrated approach that provides for disciplined, data-driven identification, selection, control, life-cycle management, and evaluation of IT investments.

In May 2000, we testified before this Subcommittee that VA had improved its processes for selecting, monitoring, and managing Capital Investment Board-level projects.[5] In addition, VA had improved its in-process and post implementation reviews. However, as we testified, the in-process reviews may still not have been timely and lessons learned from post implementation reviews were provided only to the sponsoring VA organizations, and not to decisionmakers, such as the investment panel members, who could also benefit from them. Finally, the capital investment process used for projects below the Capital Investment Board-level was not as structured, and guidance for managing those projects was not complete.

To address these issues, we testified that VA needed to (1) establish and monitor deadlines for completing in-process reviews, (2) provide decisionmakers with information on lessons learned from post implementation reviews, and (3) develop and implement guidance to better manage IT projects below the Capital Investment Board threshold.[6]

---

[4]*Assessing Risks and Returns: A Guide for Evaluating Federal Agencies' IT Investment Decision-making* (GAO/AIMD-10.1.13, February 1997).

[5]Capital Investment Board projects are those that exceed specific dollar thresholds or that are seen as high risk or high visibility. The dollar thresholds for VHA, VBA, NCA, and staff offices are acquisition costs of $10 million, $2 million, $1 million, and $1 million, respectively, and/or life-cycle costs of $30 million, $6 million, $3 million, and $3 million, respectively.

[6]GAO/T-AIMD-00-74, May 11, 2000.

Last month we recommended that the Acting Secretary of Veterans Affairs implement these actions to improve VA's IT investment decision-making process.[7] VA concurred with these recommendations, and stated that

- the in-process review plans will include completion dates,

- post implementation review findings, such as lessons learned, will be provided to investment panel members, and

- the *VA Information Technology Capital Investment Guide,* which was printed and distributed to VA's agencies earlier this month, provides guidance on processes for selecting, controlling, and evaluating IT investments and procurements below the Capital Investment Board threshold.

History and Current Status of Effort to Appoint a Chief Information Officer

The Clinger-Cohen Act directs the heads of major federal agencies to appoint CIOs to promote improvements in work processes used by the agencies to carry out their programs; implement integrated agencywide information technology architectures; and help establish sound investment review processes to select, control, and evaluate IT spending. To help ensure that these responsibilities are effectively executed, the act requires that the CIO's primary responsibility be related to information management.

In July 1998, we reported that the responsibilities of VA's CIO were not limited to information management.[8] Specifically, the CIO served the department in a variety of top management positions, including assistant secretary for management, chief financial officer, and deputy assistant secretary for budget. We noted that in an agency as decentralized as VA, the CIO was faced with many significant information management responsibilities[9] that constituted a full-time job for any CIO. Accordingly, we recommended that the Secretary of Veterans Affairs appoint a CIO with full-time responsibility for information resources management.

---

[7]GAO/AIMD-00-226, August 16, 2000.

[8]*VA Information Technology: Improvements Needed to Implement Legislative Reforms* (GAO/AIMD-98-154, July 7, 1998).

[9]At the time, these responsibilities included ensuring that (1) VA's systems development projects would not be handicapped by incomplete architectures and (2) a sound information management review process providing systematic, data-driven means of selecting, controlling and evaluating IT projects would be institutionalized.

VA concurred with this recommendation. It decided to separate the CIO function from the chief financial officer and established the position of assistant secretary for information and technology to serve as VA's CIO. This executive branch position—assistant secretary for information and technology—has remained unfilled, however, since its creation in 1998. Instead, the principal deputy assistant secretary for information and technology served as VA's acting CIO from July 1998 until he retired on June 1, 2000. The Secretary subsequently designated an acting principal deputy assistant secretary to serve as VA's acting CIO.

VA still intends to have a departmentwide CIO. The White House just announced last week that it intends to submit a nominee to the Senate for confirmation as assistant secretary for information and technology and department CIO.

VA Does Not Plan to Develop a Departmentwide Business Process Reengineering Strategy

The Clinger-Cohen Act requires agency heads to analyze the missions of their agencies and, on the basis of the results, revise and improve the agency's mission-related administrative processes before making significant investments in supporting IT. According to our business process reengineering guide,[10] an agency should have an overall business process improvement strategy that provides a means to coordinate and integrate the various reengineering and improvement projects, set priorities, and make appropriate budgetary choices.

We reported in 1998[11] that VA had not analyzed its business processes in terms of implementing its "One VA" vision. We also pointed out that VA did not have a departmentwide business process improvement strategy specifying what reengineering and improvement projects were needed, how they were related, and how they were ranked. At that time, VA concurred with our recommendation to develop such a strategy.

This past May,[12] we testified before this Subcommittee that VA no longer planned to develop such a strategy. According to VA's assistant secretary for policy and planning, the department will, instead, rely on each of its administrations—VBA, VHA, and NCA—to reengineer its own business process. We subsequently recommended to the Acting Secretary of

---

[10]*Business Process Reengineering Assessment Guide* (GAO/AIMD-10.1.15, April 1997).

[11]GAO/AIMD-98-154, July 7, 1998.

[12]GAO/T-AIMD-00-74, May 11, 2000.

Veterans Affairs that VA reassess its decision to delegate business process reengineering to the individual administrations.[13]

VA did not concur with this recommendation. Specifically, the department stated that the administrations best understand the desired outcomes of their missions and the means to achieve them. It further stated that business process reengineering is a constantly evolving function that is not conducted in a vacuum.

We agree that the individual administrations best understand their own operations and that business process reengineering is an evolving function that does not take place in a vacuum. However, by delegating primary responsibility for reengineering to the individual administrations, each administration is able to pursue its own reengineering initiatives separate and apart from each other, rather than focusing on achieving the "One VA" vision. Accordingly, VA is less likely to achieve this vision until it develops a departmentwide business process reengineering strategy.

VA Has Yet to Develop an Integrated IT Architecture

The Clinger-Cohen Act and Office of Management and Budget guidelines direct agency CIOs to implement an architecture to provide a framework for evolving or maintaining existing IT and for acquiring new IT to achieve the agency's strategic and IT goals. Leading organizations both in the private sector and in government use systems architectures to guide mission-critical systems development and to ensure the appropriate integration of information systems through common standards.[14]

In 1997, VA adopted the National Institute of Standards and Technology (NIST) five-layer model[15] for its departmentwide IT architecture. However, as discussed in our 1998 report,[16] VA and its components had yet to define a departmentwide, integrated IT architecture. Accordingly, we recommended that VA develop a detailed implementation plan with milestones for completing such an architecture. VA concurred with this recommendation.

---

[13]GAO/AIMD-00-226, August 16, 2000.

[14]*Executive Guide: Improving Mission Performance Through Strategic Information Management and Technology—Learning From Leading Organizations* (GAO/AIMD-94-115, May 1994).

[15]The five layers are business processes, information flows and relationships, applications processing, data descriptions, and technology. This provides a framework for defining an IT architecture.

[16]GAO/AIMD-98-154, July 7, 1998.

In May 1999, VA published a departmentwide technical architecture,[17] which included a technical reference model and standards profile. This document described one layer—the technology layer—of the NIST model. VA had not documented the remaining four layers—the logical architecture—showing the business processes, information flows and relationships, applications processing, and data descriptions for the department.

Mr. Chairman, during the Subcommittee's May 11, 2000, hearing, you requested that VA provide the Subcommittee with a plan and milestones for completing the logical portion of its departmentwide IT architecture within 60 days of the hearing. The resulting two-page plan, submitted to the Subcommittee on August 25, provides a high-level discussion of VA's approach for developing a target departmentwide logical architecture and time estimates for various deliverables. According to this plan, the VA administrations are expected to develop logical architectures for their administrations.

To avoid duplicating the efforts of the administrations, VA expects the departmentwide logical architecture to focus on crosscutting issues and interdependencies. VA is obtaining contractor support to develop a detailed plan with milestones and to assist in developing this departmentwide logical architecture. VA expects this architecture to be completed within 6 months of the contract award date. In commenting on a draft of this testimony, VA stated that it expects to have the contract awarded by mid-October.

VA's strategy for developing its logical architecture will not likely result in an integrated departmentwide architecture. In fact, VA acknowledges in its plan that the architectures developed by the administrations will not provide a unified picture of the department's architecture. By allowing each administration to develop its own logical architecture, at least three separate architectures could result. To avoid this, VA needs to reassess its current strategy and work together with VBA and VHA to develop an integrated, departmentwide logical architecture, consistent with the Clinger-Cohen Act. This will help foster achievement of the "One-VA" vision.

---

[17] *VA Technical Architecture: Technical Reference Model and Standards Profile*, May 1999.

VA Lacks a Uniform Mechanism for Tracking IT Expenditures

According to *VA Directive 6000*,[18] VA officials are required to maintain complete and accurate data on all personnel and non-personnel costs associated with IT activities. Further, the *VA Capital Investment Methodology Guide* requires that project managers track expenditures against budget authorizations for IT projects. In addition, according to our IT investment management guide,[19] an important step in the IT investment control process is a disciplined process for regularly tracking each project's expenditures over time. Further, according to our IT investment guide,[20] organizations should have a uniform mechanism such as a management information system for collecting, automating, and processing data on expected versus actual outcomes, including expenditures.

Although required to maintain complete and accurate IT cost data, VA does not consistently track IT expenditures across the department. Instead, the department has delegated the responsibility for tracking expenditures for IT projects to project managers within VA's administrations and offices, leading to different tracking approaches and difficulties in readily identifying the extent of IT costs.

At the administration level, the extent of expenditure tracking varies. For example, VBA tracks IT expenditures centrally for procurements, such as hardware, software, and contract services. However, VBA does not track all regional office personnel costs associated with a project. In contrast to VBA, VHA has a decentralized process for tracking IT expenditures. Specifically, it has given responsibility for tracking more than 80 percent[21] of its IT expenditures to its 22 VISNs. However, VHA does not have a uniform mechanism for tracking IT expenditures across the administration. VHA's new CIO acknowledged the need for a system to track all expenditures associated with IT projects.

Until VA develops a uniform mechanism for tracking IT expenditures, the department will be less likely to make informed decisions on whether to modify, cancel, accelerate, or continue projects. At the same time, VA and

---

[18]*VA Information Resources Management Framework*, VA Directive 6000, September 17, 1997.

[19]*Information Technology Investment Management: A Framework for Assessing and Improving Process Maturity* (GAO/AIMD-10.1.23, Exposure Draft, May 2000, Version 1).

[20]GAO/AIMD-10.1.13, February 1997.

[21]VHA officials reported that the VISNs are responsible for about $700 million (82.5 percent) of VHA's approximately $857 million IT budget for fiscal year 2000.

its administrations may be unable to provide timely cost and budget IT information to the Congress.

To improve tracking of IT project costs, VA recently initiated several actions. First, it is developing a uniform numbering system for its capital investment projects. This system is expected to generate reports from VA's financial management system showing actual expenditures associated with those projects. However, the department has yet to establish a date for when this system will be implemented. Second, VA has recently issued draft guidance[22] directing the administrations to track actual IT expenditures. The department has not yet established a deadline for finalizing the guidance. Accordingly, the department needs to (1) establish timeframes for finalizing this draft guidance and then monitor its implementation to ensure compliance and (2) establish timeframes for implementing a uniform numbering system for its capital investment projects.

Challenges Continue for Two IT Projects

I would now like to discuss the status of VA's efforts to develop and implement VHA's Decision Support System and VBA's compensation and pension replacement project. Each is at a different stage of development and implementation, and each continues to pose challenges to VA.

DSS Utilization Continues to Vary, But Action Underway to Encourage Greater Use

VHA's Decision Support System is an executive information system designed to provide VHA managers and clinicians with data on patterns of patient care and patient health outcomes, as well as the capability to analyze resource utilization and the cost of providing health care services. VHA expects to use DSS to (1) prepare budgets for its medical centers, (2) allocate resources based on performance and workload, (3) generate productivity analyses and patient-specific costs, (4) support continual quality improvement initiatives, (5) measure outcomes-based performance and effectiveness of health care delivery processes, and (6) improve efficiency of care processes through the use of clinical practice guidelines.

By the end of October 1998, DSS had been implemented at all VA medical centers. The total VA estimated cost from fiscal year 1994 through fiscal year 1999 to develop and operate DSS was approximately $213 million. As of June 30, 2000, VA calculated that it had spent another $36 million on DSS this fiscal year.

---

[22] *VA Information Technology Capital Investment Guide.*

As we testified this past May, DSS was not being fully utilized.[23] Although cost reductions and improved clinical processes had been experienced by some VISNs and medical centers using DSS, none of the ones we contacted used DSS for all of the purposes VHA intended. The reasons given by VISNs and medical centers for not making greater use of DSS included (1) concerns about the accuracy and completeness of DSS data, (2) the need for 2 years of DSS data for budget formulation and resource allocation purposes, and (3) DSS staffing issues, including insufficient staff, staff with inadequate skills, and staff turnover.

The May 2000 responses to two questions asked by VHA's chief network officer also indicate that DSS is not being fully utilized. Specifically, in a March 15, 2000, memorandum sent by VHA's chief network officer to all VISN and medical center directors, he asked for

- specific examples describing how the use of DSS had benefited veterans at the VISN and medical centers, and

- explanations for why DSS was not being used, including identification of barriers to its use.

Regarding the first question on DSS usage, 4 of 22 VISNs—VISN 6 (Durham, North Carolina), VISN 8 (Bay Pines, Florida), VISN 20 (Portland, Oregon), and VISN 21 (San Francisco)—did not provide examples of DSS use. Further, VISN 6 and VISN 21 explicitly stated that they do not use DSS at the VISN level because they did not have reliable DSS data at the time from their medical centers.

As illustrated in figure 1, the remaining 18 VISNs provided examples of using special studies/reports and cost studies/reports to make decisions with regard to resource utilization and quality improvement. Of the 18 VISNs, two—VISN 13 (Minneapolis) and VISN 10 (Cincinnati)—cited seven or more categories of DSS use; three VISNs—VISN 14 (Omaha), VISN 18 (Phoenix), and VISN 22 (Long Beach) cited only two categories of use.

---

[23]GAO/T-AIMD-00-74, May 11, 2000.

Figure 1: Categories of DSS Use by VISNs

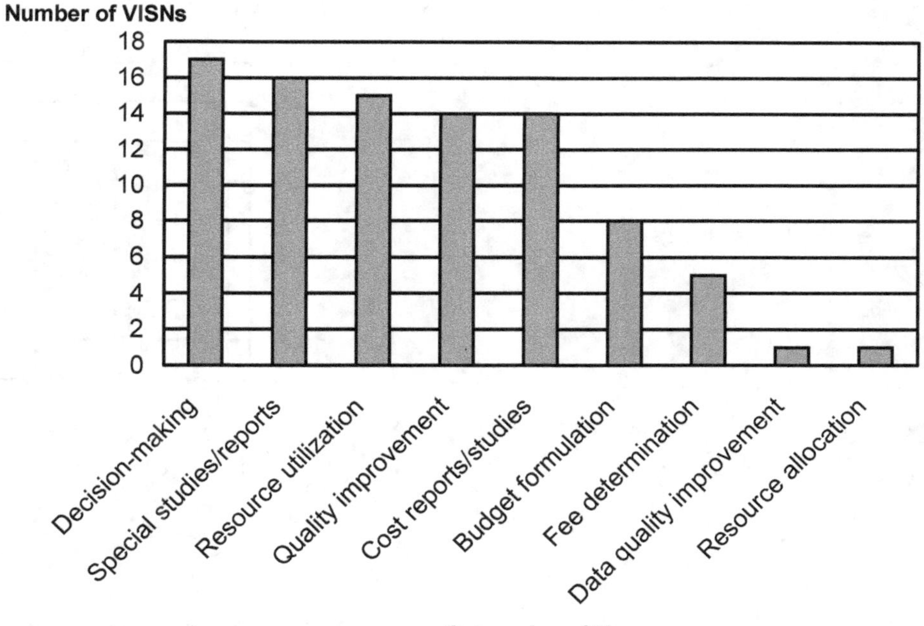

Number of VISNs

Categories of Use

Note: Eighteen VISNs provided examples of DSS use. This figure depicts the types of uses, not the quantity.

Source: GAO analysis of VISN responses.

Regarding medical centers, 59 of 140 did not provide specific examples of DSS use.[24] Three of the 59 medical centers—Beckley (West Virginia), Anchorage Health Care System, and Boise (Idaho)—explicitly stated that they did not use DSS. Both Anchorage and Boise medical centers cited staffing problems as a reason for not using DSS; Beckley indicated problems with DSS data integrity.

Figure 2 provides a snapshot of the 81 medical centers providing specific examples of DSS use. The Long Beach and Portland (Oregon) medical centers used DSS for the most categories—that is, eight or more. At the same time, three medical centers—Tomah (Wisconsin), St. Louis, and Wichita (Kansas)—cited only one category of use.

---

[24]These 59 medical centers did not provide specific examples of DSS use in their response to the March 2000 memorandum. This does not necessarily mean that they were not using DSS.

GAO/T-AIMD-00-321

Figure 2: Categories of DSS Use by Medical Centers

Number of medical centers

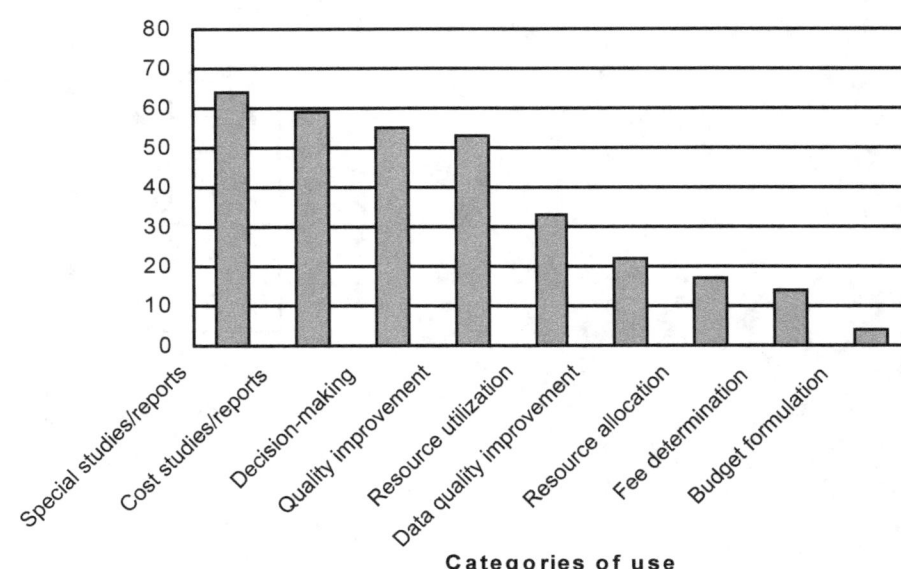

Categories of use

Note: Eighty-one medical centers provided examples of DSS use. This figure depicts the types of uses, not the quantity.

Source: GAO analysis of medical center responses.

Moving to the second question, on barriers, slightly over half of the VISNs—13—identified barriers to using DSS. As illustrated in figure 3, the barrier most often cited was the fiscal year conversion process,[25] followed by data integrity concerns, software/connectivity issues,[26] and staffing issues. Of the 24 medical centers identifying barriers, the fiscal year conversion process was also cited most frequently. For a snapshot of their responses, see figure 4.

---

[25]The conversion process entails closing out the financial and medical records for the fiscal year and establishing the structure for the new fiscal year. For fiscal year 2000, the process included a new national method to capture vendor-provided home/community health care workload, a new Veterans Health Information Systems and Technology Architecture extract that records mental health psychological testing workload, and the capability for summarizing monthly VA Denver Distribution Center costs by veteran social security number. Because of problems experienced during the fiscal year 2000 conversion process, clinical processing information did not begin until February 29, 2000.

[26]These included problems with computer crashes at the VA Austin Automation Center and problems with software enhancements.

Figure 3: Barriers to using DSS identified by VISNs

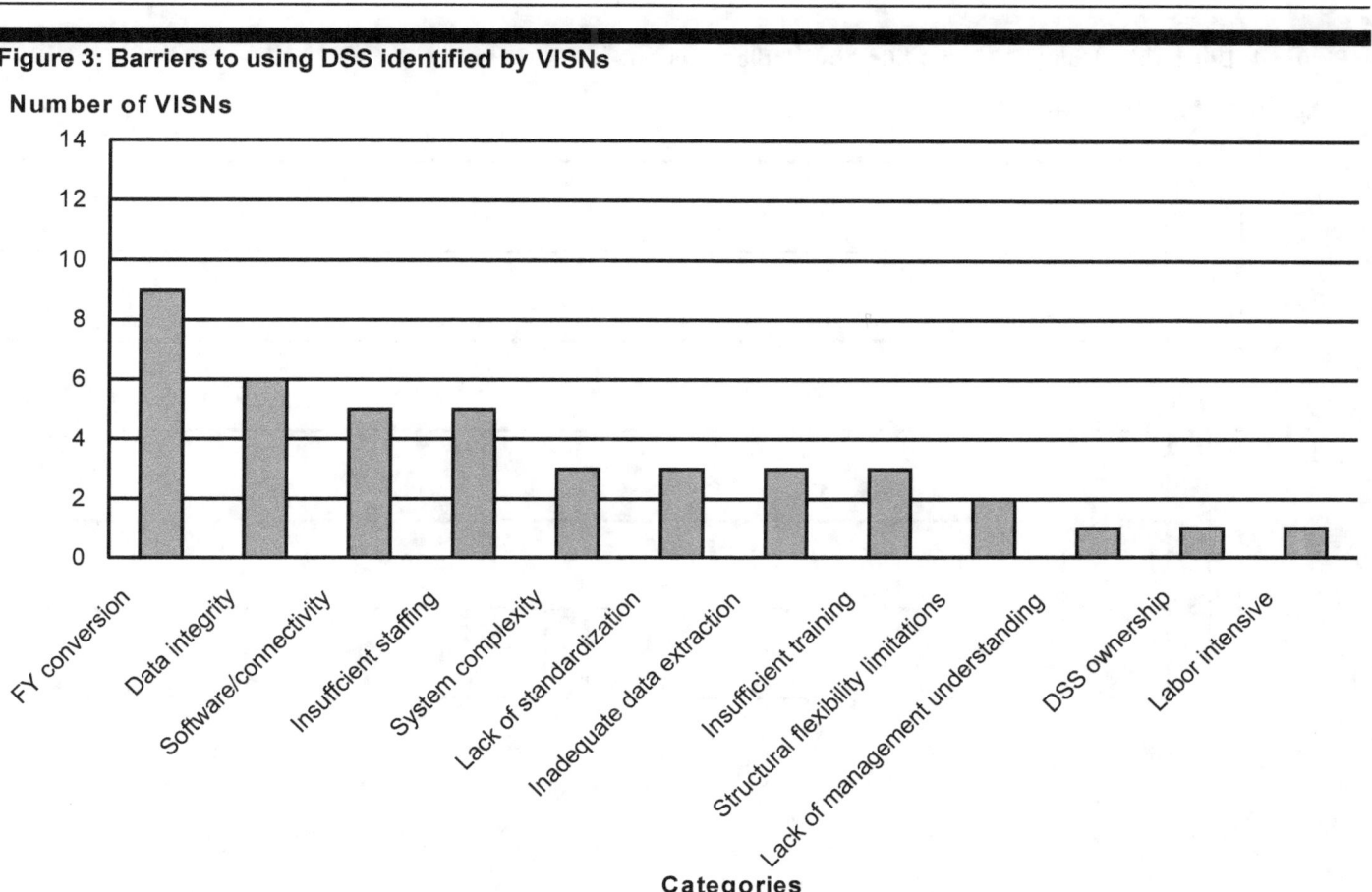

Number of VISNs

Categories

Note: Thirteen VISNs identified barriers to using DSS.

Source: GAO analysis of VISN responses.

GAO/T-AIMD-00-321

Figure 4: Barriers to Using DSS Identified by Medical Centers

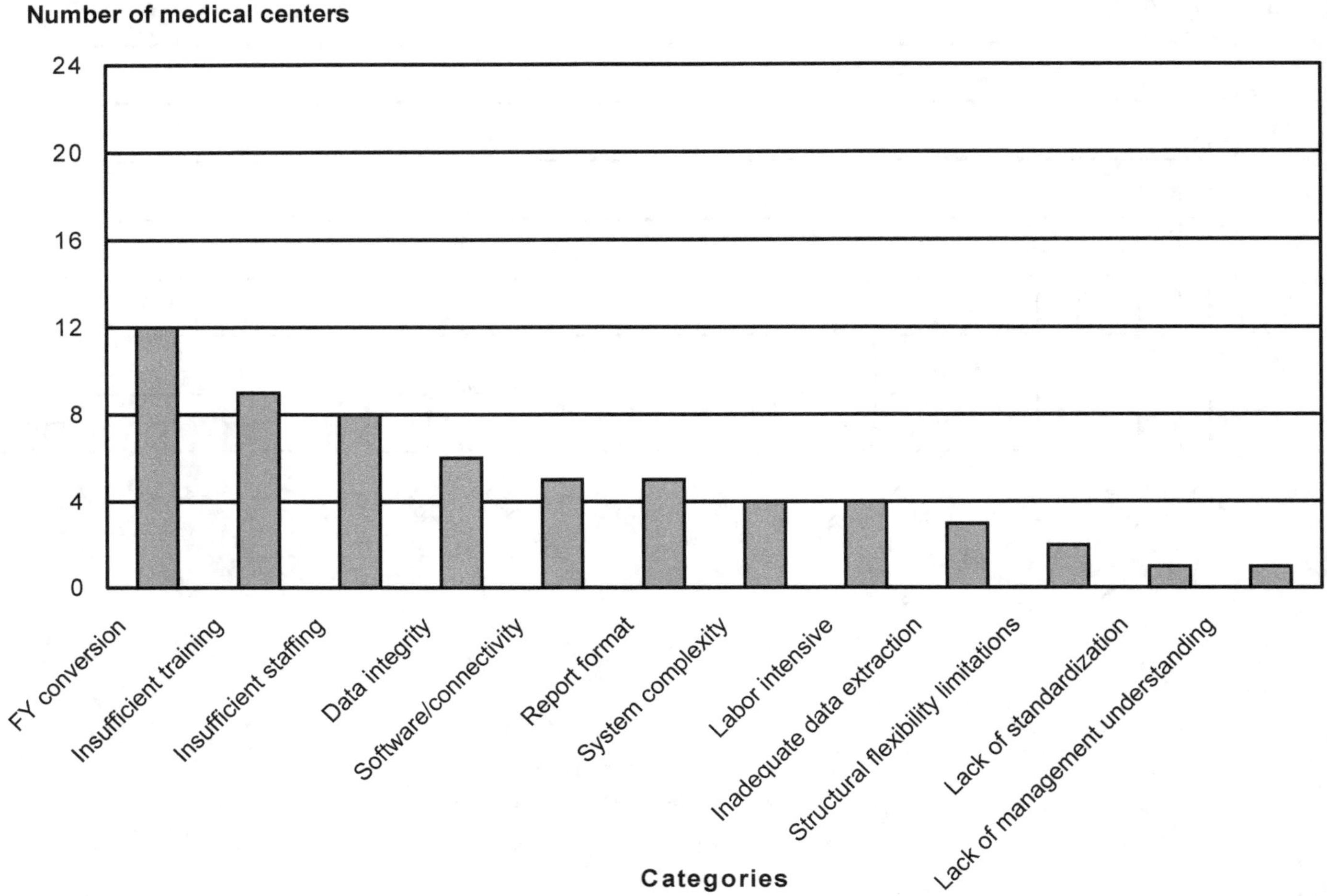

Number of medical centers

Categories

Note: Twenty-four medical centers identified barriers to using DSS.

Source: GAO analysis of medical center responses.

To address barriers with the fiscal year conversion process, the 2001 fiscal year clinical and financial conversion guidelines were issued on July 27, 2000, and the goal is to begin fiscal year 2001 processing by December 18, 2000.

Initiatives Underway to Encourage Greater Use of DSS

To encourage greater use of DSS, VHA has initiatives underway. For example, in December 1999, the undersecretary for health mandated the use of DSS data rather than data in cost distribution reports for the fiscal year 2002 budget resource allocations. DSS data will also be used as a performance measure in 2001 to determine whether VHA providers are following clinical guidelines for diabetes, according to VHA's Chief Quality and Performance Officer. Finally, the VISN and medical center managers' use of DSS data is expected to be monitored in 2001.

Even with these initiatives, VHA officials within the Office of the Associate CIO for Implementation and Training and the VISNs and medical centers have told us that they are concerned that the recent decision to move the DSS program office from the Office of the CIO to the Office of the Chief Financial Officer may diminish DSS use for clinical purposes.[27] These officials are concerned that this move may shift top management support and commitment more to the financial rather than clinical benefits of using DSS. According to VHA officials, using DSS for clinical purposes is very important and allows VA to improve health care delivery to veterans. For example, as we testified in May,[28] the clinical practice of routinely ordering two units of pre-surgery autologous[29] blood for total knee replacement was changed, based on DSS data, at the Portland (Oregon) VA medical center, resulting in estimated savings of $600+ per case.

The transition plan for moving the DSS program office is currently being drafted and will address the oversight roles and responsibilities for DSS. The plan is expected to be completed by the end of this month.

Compensation and Pension Replacement Project Remains a Challenge

The second of the two projects you asked us to review is VBA's compensation and pension replacement project, one of the major initiatives under the agency's Veterans Service Network (VETSNET) strategy. This project was intended to replace VBA's existing

---

[27]The move to the Office of the Chief Financial Officer is effective October 1, 2000.

[28]GAO/T-AIMD-00-74, May 11, 2000.

[29]Autologous (a patient's own) blood is provided by the patient in advance of surgery.

compensation and pension payment systems with one new, state-of-the-art system. The project, which began in April 1996, had an estimated cost of $8 million and was originally scheduled for completion in May 1998.

Over the years, we and others have reported on the problems VBA has encountered in completing this project.[30] We stated that one key reason for the project's delays was the lack of an integrated architecture defining the business processes, information flows and relationships, business requirements, and data descriptions. For example, the project was begun before VBA had fully developed its business requirements. Project delays subsequently resulted due to confusion over the specific requirements to be addressed.

Another reason for the project's problems was VBA's immature software development capability. In 1996 we reported that VBA's software development capability was ad hoc and chaotic—the lowest level of software development capability.[31] At this level, VBA could not reliably develop and maintain high-quality software on any major project within cost and schedule constraints. Reviews by VA and by us illustrated that this project had difficulties meeting deadlines and that not all critical systems development areas were addressed. To date, VBA has yet to reach the next, repeatable, level of software development.

The compensation and pension replacement project has missed several key milestones. For example, the project missed its original May 1998 completion date and a revised completion date of December 1998. In 1999, VBA changed its strategy for the compensation and pension replacement project to incorporate several software products previously developed and used at selected VBA regional offices. At that time, VBA did not have a completion date for this project.

Since then, VBA has developed short-term milestones for this project. Specifically, the first product scheduled for implementation under VBA's revised strategy is expected to be rating board automation 2000. This product is expected to be implemented this November and is to assist veterans service representatives in rating benefit claims. Other products

---

[30]*Veterans Benefits Modernization: Management and Technical Weaknesses Must Be Overcome if Modernization Is To Succeed* (GAO/T-AIMD-96-103, June 19, 1996), *Veterans Benefits Computer Systems: Risks of VBA's Year 2000 Program* (GAO/AIMD-97-79, May 30, 1997), *and VETSNET Quarterly Review*, Office of Information Resources Management, Department of Veterans Affairs, March 1998.

[31]Software Capability Evaluation: VA's Software Development Process Is Immature (GAO/AIMD-96-90, June 19, 1996) and GAO/T-AIMD-96-103.

under development as part of the compensation and pension replacement project include:

- Modern award processing-development (MAP-D)—which is expected to manage claims development processes, including the collection of data to support the claim, requests for exams to determine degree of injury or disability, and tracking of the claim. MAP-D is also expected to provide direct access to three other software products that address claims development processes.

- Search/participant profile—which is expected to establish the veteran record and collect basic information on the veteran and family.

- Award processing—which is expected to compute the award or payment amount based on the results of the rating process.

- Finance and accounting system—which is expected to develop the actual payment record and handle all accounting functions.

The project manager said that current plans are to complete development and testing of these five products by December 2000. A pilot test of all of the above products except MAP-D is expected to begin in January 2001. In the pilot, 10 new claims are to be processed and payments generated using the new products.

However, before the compensation and pension replacement pilot can be fully implemented, top management in VBA must address several important issues. First, large, complex projects, such as the compensation and pension replacement project should have an approved project management plan and schedule to determine what needs to be done and when, and to use as a means of measuring progress. VBA has yet to develop such a project plan and schedule for developing and implementing this system. Instead, detailed plans and schedules exist only for the next few months.

Similarly, VBA has yet to address fully other critical systems development areas. The first of these is data conversion. Specifically, data in the existing VBA system will need to be converted to the new system. According to VBA officials, this is the most difficult remaining part of the compensation and pension replacement project. They told us that a data conversion strategy has been drafted and is under review.

In addition, VBA must develop data exchanges to allow the compensation and pension replacement system to share data with other systems. For example, it is critical that changes to veteran information, such as name and address, captured in the compensation and pension replacement system be changed in other VBA systems.

Lastly, VBA is vulnerable to disruptions due to contractor volatility and staffing uncertainties. For example, of the 25 contractors currently involved in the compensation and pension replacement project, over half (13) have been added to the project within the last year. According to VBA officials, they may also experience problems with obtaining in-house staff from its data centers to help develop the compensation and pension replacement system and other VBA projects, such as an effort to consolidate VBA's data center operations from Hines (Illinois) and Philadelphia to Austin, because they compete for some of the same people over the next 2 years. These concerns increase the likelihood that schedule delays and cost overruns may occur.

VBA officials acknowledge the above issues and have informed us that efforts are underway to address them. However, until VBA develops a fully integrated project plan and schedule that incorporates all critical system development areas, challenges and vulnerabilities will remain.

VA Continues to Address Computer Security Challenges

The last area you asked us to discuss is computer security—critical to any organization's ability to safeguard its assets, maintain the confidentiality of sensitive information, and ensure the reliability of its financial data. If effective computer security practices are not in place, financial and sensitive information contained in VA's systems is at risk of inadvertent or deliberate misuse, fraud, improper disclosure, or destruction—possibly occurring without detection.

Over the past several years we have reported on VA's computer security weaknesses. In September 1998 we reported that computer security weaknesses placed critical VA operations such as financial management, health care delivery, and benefits payments at risk of misuse and disruption.[32] We reported in October 1999 that VA's success in improving computer security largely depended on strong commitment and adequate resources being dedicated to the information security program plan.[33] In May 2000 we testified[34] that VA had still not adequately limited the access

---

[32]*Information Systems: VA Computer Control Weaknesses Increase Risk of Fraud, Misuse, and Improper Disclosure* (GAO/AIMD-98-175, September 23, 1998).

[33]Information Systems: The Status of Computer Security at the Department of Veterans Affairs (GAO/AIMD-00-5, October 4, 1999).

[34]GAO/T-AIMD-00-74.

granted to authorized users, appropriately segregated incompatible duties among computer personnel, adequately managed user identification and passwords, or routinely monitored access activity.

Earlier this month, we reported that serious computer security problems persisted throughout the department and VHA because VA had not yet fully implemented an integrated security management program and VHA had not effectively managed computer security at its medical facilities.[35] Consequently, financial transaction data and personal information on veterans' medical records continued to face increased risk of inadvertent or deliberate misuse, fraudulent use, improper disclosure, or destruction. Specifically, as we reported, VA's New Mexico, North Texas, and Maryland health care systems had not adequately controlled access granted to authorized users, prevented employees from performing incompatible duties, secured access to networks, restricted physical access to computer resources, or ensured the continuation of computer processing operations in case of unexpected interruption.

To facilitate VA actions to develop and implement a comprehensive, coordinated security management program that would encompass VHA and other VA organizations, we reiterated our October 1999 recommendation that VA develop computer security guidance and oversight processes and recommended that VA monitor and resolve coordination issues that could affect the success of the departmentwide computer security program.

VA concurred with these recommendations and stated that it intends to develop an accelerated plan to improve information security at its facilities. Specifically, VA stated that it would track the resolution of the recommendations we made to correct specific information security weaknesses at the health care systems we visited. In addition, VA provided examples of security management activities performed by the VHA central security group to implement and oversee computer security throughout the administration. VA also stated that it would use its Information Security Working Group, which includes representatives of all administration and staff office security groups, to develop departmentwide policy, guidance, and processes.

---

[35] *VA Information Systems: Computer Security Weaknesses Persist at the Veterans Health Administration* (GAO/AIMD-00-232, September 8, 2000).

GAO/T-AIMD-00-321

In summary, the department still faces important challenges in several IT areas. While it has improved its IT investment decision-making process and plans to fill its department CIO position, VA may encounter problems achieving its "One VA" vision until it develops an overall business process reengineering strategy and a departmentwide, integrated IT architecture. Full implementation of our prior recommendations in these areas is essential to VA's achieving its "One VA" vision. In addition, VA's lack of departmentwide tracking of IT expenditures makes it difficult for the department to manage the risks of its IT investments. Further, top management support and commitment are essential to addressing the challenges VA faces in making greater use of DSS and in addressing issues involved in developing the compensation and pension replacement project. Improving VA's computer security will also take sustained leadership and commitment to developing and implementing a comprehensive security management program.

We performed this assignment in accordance with generally accepted government auditing standards, from June through September 2000. In carrying out this assignment, we assessed the actions taken to address our recommendations on improving VA's IT investment decision-making process. We reviewed documentation on VA's efforts to fill the CIO position and reviewed and analyzed VA, VBA, and VHA IT architecture documents, comparing these with NIST's five-layer standard, the guidance used by VA. To determine how IT expenditures are tracked, we reviewed and analyzed VA's policies and procedures and compared them with applicable guidance in this area. We discussed cost tracking procedures with officials at VA, VBA, VHA, and five VISNs, and reviewed relevant documentation.

For the DSS project, we reviewed VISN and medical center examples for DSS use and barriers, and visited four VISNs—VISN 5 (Baltimore), VISN 8 (Bay Pines, Florida), VISN 18 (Phoenix), and VISN 21 (San Francisco)—to discuss their examples of DSS use and barriers to such use. Specifically, we analyzed the examples provided by the VISNs and medical centers and summarized them into nine categories of DSS use and 13 categories of barriers to such use. We also reviewed performance documentation and met with VHA officials to discuss actions planned for DSS use. For the compensation and pension replacement project, we reviewed plans and schedules for the project and visited the development site at Bay Pines. We also discussed issues with VBA managers in Washington, D.C. In the area of computer security, we evaluated security controls at three VHA medical facilities—VA Maryland Health Care System, VA New Mexico Health Care System, and the VA North Texas Health Care System—and reviewed our recent reports and VA updates on actions taken to address our recommendations.

We provided a draft of this testimony to VA for comments and incorporated changes where appropriate.

Mr. Chairman, this concludes my statement. I would be pleased to respond to any questions that you or other members of the Subcommittee may have at this time.

Contact and Acknowledgments

For information about this testimony, please contact me at (202) 512-6253 or by e-mail at *willemssenj.aimd@gao.gov*. Individuals making key contributions to this testimony included Nabajyoti Barkakati, Michael P. Fruitman, Amanda Gill, Tonia L. Johnson, Helen Lew, Barbara S. Oliver, J. Michael Resser, and Kevin Secrest.

(511856)